ULTIMATE ✦ SPECIAL FORCES

US MARINE CORPS

TIM COOKE

PowerKiDS
press™

New York

Published in 2013 by The Rosen Publishing Group, Inc.
29 East 21st Street, New York, NY 10010

Senior Editor: Tim Cooke
US Editor: Sara Antill
Designer: Supriya Sahai
Picture Researcher: Andrew Webb
Creative Director: Jeni Child
Picture Manager: Sophie Mortimer
Children's Publisher: Anne O'Daly
Production Director: Alastair Gourlay
Editorial Director: Lindsey Lowe

Picture credits
Front Cover: US Marine Corps
Library of Congress: 22, 23tl, 23b, 24/25, 25tr; National Archives: 04, 05tr, 05bl; Robert Hunt Library: 14, 16, 17, 18, 19, 20, 21, 26; US Department of Defense: 10, 11, 12, 13, 15, 27, 28, 29t, 29br, 30, 31tr, 31bl, 32, 34, 35, 36, 37, 38/39, 40; US Marine Corps: 33, 39tr, 41, 42, 43tl, 43b, 44, 45; US Navy: 06, 07, 08, 09.
Key: t = top, c = center, b = bottom, l = left, r = right.

Library of Congress Cataloging-in-Publication Data

Cooke, Tim, 1961–
 US Marine Corps / by Tim Cooke.
     p. cm. — (Ultimate special forces)
 Includes index.
 ISBN 978-1-4488-7880-2 (library binding) — ISBN 978-1-4488-7957-1 (pbk.) — ISBN 978-1-4488-7962-5 (6-pack)
 1. United States. Marine Corps—Juvenile literature. I. Title.
 VE23.C738 2013
 359.9'60973—dc23

2012008232

Manufactured in the United States of America

CPSIA Compliance Information: Batch #B2S12PK: For further information, contact Rosen Publishing, New York, New York, at 1-800-237-9932.

CONTENTS

INTRODUCTION

November 10 is a special day for the United States Marine Corps (USMC). That's the day in 1775, during the Revolutionary War, when Samuel Nicholas of Philadelphia created two battalions of marines to serve as infantry for the new US Navy.

THESE MARINES served the Union army during the Civil War.

EYEWITNESS

"We are United States Marines, and for two and a quarter centuries we have defined the standards of courage, esprit, and military prowess."

General James L. Jones
Commandant of the Marine Corps, November 10, 2000

MARINES storm the palace of Chapultepec, in Mexico City, during the Mexican-American War (1846–1848).

PROUD HISTORY

Since then, the Marines have taken part in every US conflict. Their proud history includes some of the most famous battles in US history, like the capture of Iwo Jima from the Japanese in 1945. During the Vietnam War (1965–1975), Marines defended a base at Khe Sanh for months. The Marines are proud of their motto, "Semper fidelis," which means "always faithful." And they've adopted a second one, "Once a Marine, always a Marine."

A RECRUITING poster from World War I (1914–1918) calls for volunteers to enlist in the US Marines.

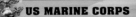
MARINES drill on board an assault ship.

ORGANIZATION

The Marine Corps is smaller than the Army, Navy, or Air Force. But that doesn't mean it's not powerful. Its role is as a rapid-reaction force. It's ready to go to trouble spots around the world at a moment's notice. Although it is run by the Department of the Navy, the Marine Corps operates as a self-contained unit.

THE MARINE CORPS is part of the Department of the Navy.

COMPETITION

The USMC operates as an army within an army, which isn't always popular with the US Army. The USMC has the hardware it needs to operate immediately and alone. The two services are fiercely competitive.

"RULE OF THREE"

The Marines love multiples of three. Their basic unit is the fire team, which is made up of three men plus a team leader. Three fire teams make a rifle squad. Three rifle squads make a platoon. Three platoons make a company (or battery). Three companies make a battalion, three battalions a regiment (or brigade). Three brigades make a division. Each grouping also has its own leadership.

FORMAL DRILL, like this Sunset Parade, is a proud part of Marine tradition.

BOOT CAMP

What separates Marines from other soldiers? Training. In the Army, basic training lasts eight weeks; in the Marines, it lasts twelve. Basic training, called boot camp, is hard. Drill instructors intimidate new recruits (or poolees) to simulate the stress of conflict. They teach recruits not to think of themselves as individuals. A recruit also has to pass fitness tests, including running 1.5 miles (2.4 km) in 13.5 minutes.

POOLEES for boot camp have their first encounter with a drill instructor.

A RECRUIT struggles with push-ups on sloping bars.

EYEWITNESS

"A Marine is a Marine. You're a Marine, just in a different uniform and you're in a different phase of your life. But you'll always be a Marine because you went to Parris Island, San Diego, or the hills of Quantico. There's no such thing as a former Marine."

General James F. Amos
35th Commandant of the Marine Corps

INTO THE CRUCIBLE

The climax of boot camp is the Crucible. For 54 hours, recruits live in simulated combat conditions, with minimum food and sleep. They face challenges that test their training, including rifle marksmanship, martial arts, and patrols that cover a total of 48 miles (77 km). But the recruits are tough: the drill instructors get about 90 percent of them through boot camp and the Crucible to become Marines.

THE BASIC SCHOOL

A THREE-MAN crew of officer trainees fire an M240 during an exercise at The Basic School.

Marine officers spend six months at The Basic School in Quantico, Virginia. The course combines classroom and field exercises and tough physical demands. During training, recruits adopt an occupational specialty, from joining the military police to flying a helicopter.

AN INSTRUCTOR demonstrates how to use an assault pack as a flotation device to keep a rifle above the water.

FIVE HORIZONTAL THEMES

The Five Horizontal Themes define the kind of officer the Marines need. Up to 50 percent of recruits at Quantico don't make the grade.

- A man or woman of exemplary character.
- Devoted to leading Marines 24/7.
- Able to decide, communicate, and act in the fog of war,
- A warfighter who embraces the Corps' warrior ethos.
- Mentally strong and physically tough.

CORE VALUES

Recruits learn the core values of the Marine Officer Corps:

Honor—respect others, act responsibly.

Courage—face fears and overcome them.

Commitment—determination and dedication of each Marine.

UNARMED COMBAT

A key part of Marine training is CQC: close-quarter combat. It's the most ancient form of fighting, but the Marines use the most modern techniques of martial arts. They learn to fight unarmed or with small weapons, rifles, daggers, and even bayonets.

STUDENT officers at The Basic School follow the Martial Arts Program.

FEMALE MARINES wrestle as preparation to work at checkpoints in Iraq.

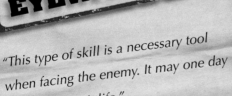

EYEWITNESS

"This type of skill is a necessary tool when facing the enemy. It may one day save a Marine's life."

Bill Miller
Sergeant, USMC, and Korean War Veteran

MARTIAL ARTS

The MCMAP—Marine Corps Martial Arts Program—brings together the best parts of different martial arts: judo, karate, jujitsu, and kickboxing. It enables a Marine to fight effecively, whether he or she weighs 220 pounds (100 kg) or just 110 pounds (50 kg). A lot of the program is about mental discipline. The Marines study warriors such as ninja or the Apache to see how they fought.

THE FEW, THE PROUD

Marines are taught that joining the USMC is more than a job. They have joined a privileged elite for life. They are Marines 24/7. Marine regulations even restrict what clothes they can wear off duty. Being a Marine doesn't end with retirement from active service. Marines swear lifelong loyalty to their fellow Marines and to the Corps they serve.

MARINES raise the flag on Iwo Jima during World War II. The victory was one of their most famous ever.

EYEWITNESS

"I love the Corps for those intangible possessions that cannot be issued: pride, honor, integrity, and being able to carry on the traditions for generations of warriors past."

Jeff Sornig
Corporal, USMC,
November 1994

A PLACE IN HISTORY

Every Marine appreciates the USMC history and his or her place in it. That's why their recruiting slogan is "The Few. The Proud." They train longer and harder than the regular Army. There are fewer of them. But they have fought in battles that have changed US history. Even their nickname, the Leathernecks, is historical. It comes from the late 18th century, when they wore leather collars to protect their necks.

A MARINE band marches in a Columbus Day parade. The Marines take their traditions very seriously.

WORLD WAR II

1941–1945

PACIFIC OCEAN

Ontong Java Atoll

Choiseul

Santa Isabel

SOLOMON ISLANDS

Malaita

Honiara

Guadalcanal

Duff Islands

Reef Islands

Santa Cruz Islands

Solomon Sea

Makira

Nendo

Utupua

Vanikoro

Rennell

The Marines and the Navy led the Pacific campaign against Japan after the attack on Pearl Harbor on December 7, 1941. The US strategy was to get closer to Japan by crossing the Pacific. The Marines carried out a series of amphibious landings to capture islands that acted as "stepping stones."

GUADACANAL, in the Solomon Islands, was a key stepping stone for the US advance.

MARINES come ashore from a landing craft at Guadalcanal on August 7, 1942.

FIGHT AT GUADALCANAL

On Guadacanal, part of the Solomon Islands, 10,000 Marines carried out the first large US amphibious operation of the war on August 7, 1942. The battle against the Japanese would last six months. The Marines fought in terrible conditions. Many got really sick, their clothes rotted away, they never had enough to eat or enough ammunition. But in the end they wore down the Japanese to secure an important airfield for operations against Japan.

EYEWITNESS

"Casualties many. Percentage of dead not known. Combat efficiency, we are winning."

David M. Shoup
USMC colonel at Tarawa, 1943

"You'll never get the Purple Heart hiding in a foxhole! Follow me!"

Henry P. "Jim" Crowe
USMC captain, Guadalcanal

MARINES shelter under fire on the beach on the island of Peleliu, September 15, 1944.

ISLAND-HOPPING
1943–1945

MAP OF JAPAN

The Pacific campaign included some of the Marines' most famous battles. At "Terrible Tarawa," 5,000 Marines captured the island but lost more than 50 percent casualties. There were other costly victories at Peleliu and the Marianas Islands. As the Americans got closer to Japan itself, resistance grew fiercer. Enemy soldiers and even civilians killed themselves rather than surrender.

THE CAPTURE of Okinawa brought US Forces within striking distance of Japan itself.

ON OKINAWA Marines take aim at an entrenched enemy.

EYEWITNESS

"The 3rd, 4th and 5th Marine Divisions and other units of the Fifth Amphibious Corps have made an accounting to their country which only history will be able to value fully. Among the Americans who served on Iwo Island, uncommon valor was a common virtue."

Admiral Chester W. Nimitz, Commander in Chief, US Pacific Fleet

MARINES wade through 3 feet (1 m) of surf at Cape Gloucester, New Britain, in December 1943.

FINAL VICTORIES

At Iwo Jima, Marines were pinned down on beaches of black volcanic ash. But their superior numbers eventually won out. Virtually all of the 18,000 Japanese defenders, were killed; 6,821 Marines died. The last amphibious landing of the campaign was also the biggest: at Okinawa, more than 80,000 Marines and 100,000 Army soldiers fought for 82 days to secure victory.

KOREA

1950–1953

War broke out in 1950 between communist-backed North Korea and United Nations (UN) forces. US Marines made a surprise landing at Inchon to relieve Seoul, in South Korea. They borrowed landing craft and went ashore with close fighter support. The battle was a huge victory for the Marines.

MAP OF SOUTH KOREA

NORTH KOREA

Paengnyong

Seoul

Inch'on

SOUTH KOREA

Han

Ulung

Yellow Sea

Kum

Taejon

Sea of Japan

Naktong

Taegu

Ulsan

Kwangju

Pusan

Cheju

Korea Strait

Tsushima (Japan)

JAPAN

THE WAR in Korea ended with the division of the peninsula into North and South Korea.

USING LADDERS
Marines go over the top after landing at Inchon in the campaign to relieve Seoul.

A MARINE COMPANY follows its armor through the snow around the Chosin Reservoir.

RESISTANCE AT CHOSIN

When the Chinese entered Korea from the north, many UN and US forces retreated. The Marines held their positions. At Chosin Reservoir, the 1st Marine Division was surrounded by the Chinese, outnumbered 8-to-1. They marched across harsh terrain. They froze as temperatures fell to -40°F (-40°C). They didn't sleep or eat much. However, they eventually fought off the enemy.

EYEWITNESS

"We've been looking for the enemy for days. We've finally found them. We are surrounded. They're on our left, they're on our right, they're in front of us, they're behind us. They can't get away this time."

Lewis B. "Chesty" Puller
USMC colonel, Chosin Reservoir, Korea, 1950

VIETNAM
1961–1975

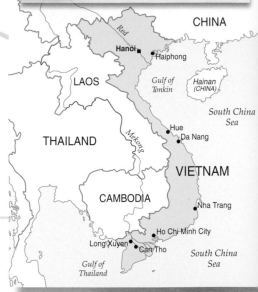

CHINA

Red

Hanoi — Haiphong

LAOS

Gulf of Tonkin — Hainan (CHINA)

South China Sea

THAILAND

Mekong

Hue
Da Nang

VIETNAM

CAMBODIA

Nha Trang

Ho Chi Minh City

Long Xuyen — Can Tho

Gulf of Thailand

South China Sea

When Marine advisors first went to Vietnam in 1964, war was raging between the United States, South Vietnam, and the North Vietnamese. The Marines hoped to win the hearts and minds of local people. Instead they found themselves fighting a search-and-destroy war.

WEARY Marines rest during a bombardment at Khe Sanh.

EYEWITNESS

"We discovered that wherever there weren't bomb craters, there were bunkers. The NVA [North Vietnamese Army] had reoccupied some of these very bunkers and had been rooted out again in an eight-hour fight. Many of them were filled with dead (now putrefact) NVA and their gear."

James Epp
USMC, Khe Sanh

THE BASE at Khe Sanh was only accessible by air so all supplies were flown in.

KHE SANH SIEGE

Khe Sanh was a remote combat base in the hills near Laos. In 1967 6,000 Marines were surrounded there by more than 17,000 enemy fighters. The North Vietnamese anticipated an easy victory. They bombarded the base with artillery. They threw attack after attack at its perimeter and its outposts in the nearby hills. But the Marines and their South Vietnamese allies held out for 77 days until they were relieved. Khe Sanh was later abandoned, but only on US terms.

A MARINE uses a flamethrower to clear ground at Khe Sanh.

HUE CITY

1968

LAOS
Gulf of Tonkin
Hainan (CHINA)
South China Sea
THAILAND
Mekong
Hue
Da Nang
VIETNAM

Fighting house-to-house is dangerous. But that's how Marines had to retake Hue in central Vietnam in 1968 after the North Vietnamese Army (NVA) seized it in a suprise operation. Many of the Marines facing the NVA had never been in combat before. Even the veterans had no experience in urban fighting.

MARINES prepare to advance during the close-quarter fighting in Hue City.

A MARINE machine-gun crew opens up during an enemy offensive in January 1968.

EYEWITNESS

"We found that by 0700 hours [the building] was heavily occupied. We were trying to secure the church, and the enemy was inside the school next door. We had to blow holes in the walls so we could get through and take the school rooms. It was very tough fighting."

Ray Smith
Alpha Company, USMC,
Hue City

TOWARD THE CITADEL

The NVA had turned houses and stores into fortresses. The buildings were booby-trapped. Snipers lay in wait and machine gunners lurked in the rubble. The Marines had to clear the city building by building, street by street. Most of the time they fought without air support: Hue was home to many historic buildings that the US Air Force did not want to damage. It took a month's fighting to reach the citadel at the heart of the city and drive out the last NVA.

CENTRAL AMERICA

1980s

MAP OF PANAMA

Caribbean Sea

COSTA RICA

L Gatún • Colón L Bayano
La Chorrera • **Panama City**
David • PANAMA • Penonomé
• Santiago
• Las Tablas

Gulf of Panama

COLOMBIA

PACIFIC OCEAN

In the 1980s, Marines were sent into their own backyard. In Panama, General Manuel Noriega had made himself dictator. But the US controlled the Panama Canal Zone, and US citizens lived there. Operation Just Cause was launched to protect the Panama Canal in 1989.

MARINES patrol a street in Grenville, Grenada, looking for enemy fighters.

GET THE GENERAL

The Marine Corps Security Force, infantry, and a Fleet Antiterrorism Security Team (FAST) had a critical role. Their brief was to depose General Noriega himself. Fighting house-to-house in the capital, Panama City, Marines overcame all resistance from Noriega's supporters in two weeks. Only one Marine died in the operation. Noriega was arrested and democracy was restored to Panama.

URGENT FURY

In Operation Urgent Fury, Marines invaded the Caribbean island of Grenada in 1983. They were part of a force sent to overthrow a coup. There was little resistance and the campaign lasted only five days.

TWO MARINES wait in their UH-1 Huey in Grenada for news during Operation Urgent Fury.

DESERT SHIELD

1990

MAP OF SAUDI ARABIA

When Iraqi dictator Saddam Hussein invaded Kuwait on August 2, 1990, the United States sent forces to nearby Saudi Arabia. A task force of amphibious ships carried US Marines to the Persian Gulf. On the voyage, the Marines trained in chemical warfare and other threats they might face.

A MARINE flys the flag during an exercise in the Persian Gulf.

FAST RESPONSE

Desert Shield showed just how effective the Marines can be as a fast-response force. They had to get to Saudi Arabia fast, but it was 10,000 miles (16,000 km) away. But the task force was assembled and was underway in just 11 days.

A MARINE surveys the desert from his M998 High-Mobility Multipurpose Wheeled Vehicle (HMMWV).

POWERFUL TASK FORCE

Eventually the Marines were part of the largest amphibious force gathered for 30 years: air, land, and sea units trained for coastal assault. Air cover would be provided by attack jets and assault helicopters. Armor would be carried ashore aboard special high-speed air-cushion landing craft (LCAC). Meanwhile, the Marines helped Navy ships patrol the Gulf, boarding Iraqi oil tankers to intercept them as part of a blockade of Iraqi trade.

MARINES wear protective field masks against possible chemical attack.

DESERT STORM

1991

More Marines took part in the campaign to rid Kuwait of its Iraqi invaders than any other branch of the US military. The Marines are intended for rapid response. Unlike the Army or the Navy, they have all the gear and personnel they need, from landing craft to jet fighters. A Marine Air-Ground Task Force can be ready in days.

MAP OF KUWAIT

IRAN

IRAQ

Shatt al Arab

KUWAIT

Bubiyan

Kuwait

Failaka

Jahra

Hawalli

Ahmadi

Persian Gulf

SAUDI ARABIA

A MARINE SIGHTS with his M249 squad automatic weapon (SAW).

MARINES of the 1st Marine Expeditionary Force stream across the Saudi desert.

RAPID VICTORY

In January, an Allied air campaign began raining bombs on Iraqi forces. On February 23, the 1st Marine Division, 2nd Marine Division, and the 1st Light Armored Infantry headed into Kuwait. They faced trenches, barbed wire, and minefields, but few Iraqi soldiers. Apart from some tank battles, there was almost no resistance. Air power had convinced most of the Iraqi troops to surrender or flee.

EYEWITNESS

"It was a classic military breaching of a very, very tough minefield, barbed wire, fire trench-type barrier. They went through the first barrier like it was water. Then they brought both divisions streaming through that breach."

Norman Schwarzkopf
Commander,
Coalition Forces, Gulf War

A MARINE corporal maintains a TOW2 antitank weapon.

31

OPERATION SHARP EDGE

1990–1991

MAP OF LIBERIA

SIERRA LEONE
GUINEA
CÔTE D'IVOIRE
Mano
St Paul
St John
Monrovia
Buchanan
LIBERIA
Cavally
ATLANTIC OCEAN
Harper

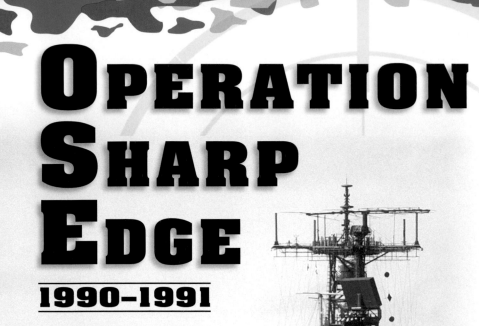

In 1989 Liberia, in West Africa, was rocked as rebel groups fought each other. When rebel leader Prince Johnson threatened to attack Americans at the US Embassy, the Marines were sent in. Their task was to rescue US diplomats and citizens from the capital city, Monrovia.

HELICOPTERS lift off the amphibious assault ship USS *Saipan* during Operation Sharp Edge in 1989.

FAST ACTION

The Marines sent to Liberia belonged to the Fleet Antiterrorism Security Team (FAST). Their job is to find and stop terrorists and to protect US embassies from terrorist attack. They are stationed at naval bases, ready to be deployed on short notice.

SUCCESSFUL RESCUE

Four warships carrying 2,300 Marines began the operation using helicopters on August 5, 1990. They reinforced the US embassy. Over the next six months, they evacuated more than 2,500 foreigners, including 330 Americans. There was no fighting. The Marines also helped Liberians caught up in the civil war: they airlifted food, water, fuel, and medical supplies.

CHILDREN run beside a Marine convoy delivering assistance to a town in Liberia.

OPERATION PHANTOM FURY 2004

MAP OF IRAQ

SYRIA

Mosul • Irbil
Sulaimaniyah
Kirkuk •

JORDAN

Baghdad

IRAQ

An Najaf • Hilla •

IRAN

Basra •

KUWAIT Persi
Gu

SAUDI ARABIA

By late 2004 the war in Iraq that began the previous year focused on hunting insurgents, rebel fighters who used guerrilla and terrorist tactics. A key base for Iraqis fighting coalition forces was Fallujah. With Iraqi and British allies, US Marines began their heaviest urban combat fighting since Vietnam.

A MARINE checks the streets of Fallujah from the turret of an M1A1 Abrams Main Battle Tank.

ARMORED FIREPOWER

Inside Fallujah up to 4,000 insurgents had dug trenches, hidden explosive devices, and planted booby traps. But they had not bargained on the Marines' hardware strength. Tanks bulldozed a route into the city, followed by four battalions of infantry. Artillery, mortars, and snipers provided back up. Fighting house-to-house, the Marines cleared Fallujah of rebels in seven hard weeks.

EYEWITNESS

"You got a very eerie feeling when you drove into that city [Fallujah]. You could see the houses, and you could just tell it was going to be an ugly fight. The Marines were ready to go—we don't like to sit around and wait."

Jeremiah Workman
USMC Sergeant, Fallujah, November 2004

ARMED WITH an M16A2 rifle, a Marine takes a rest on a patrol through Fallujah.

AFGHANISTAN

2001–2010

Marines joined Operation Enduring Freedom in October 2001. Marine Expeditionary Units (MEUs) were the first troops to back up US special forces who went into Afghanistan at the start of the invasion. They captured Kandahar airport from the enemy Taliban in December 2001.

MAP OF AFGHANISTAN

UZBEKISTAN
TAJIKISTAN
CHINA
TURKMENISTAN
Amu Darya
Mazar-i-Sharif
Kunduz
Baghlan
Herat
Hari Rud
Kabul
Kabul
Jalalabad
IRAN
AFGHANISTAN
Helmand
Kandahar
Indus
PAKISTAN
INDIA

A MARINE talks to children while on patrol in Helmand province, in Afghanistan.

MARINES patrol with Afghan soldiers after clearing Taliban from Nawa, in southern Afghanistan, in 2009.

EYEWITNESS

"You really can't prepare a Marine to lose his good buddy or see another one of his buddies with both his legs blown off. The best way to overcome that is to get right back out on a patrol the next day because it doesn't happen every time you go out."

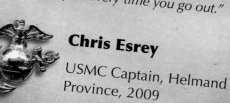

Chris Esrey

USMC Captain, Helmand Province, 2009

CONTINUING ACTION

In July 2009, 4,000 Marines from the 2nd Expeditionary Brigade carried out Operation Strike of the Sword. They used helicopters to seize control of towns dominated by the Taliban in Helmand province. The campaign was intended to reassure local people that the new Iraqi government was in charge. After a week of fighting, the Taliban drifted out of the area, leaving the Marines in charge.

AIRCRAFT

A Marine Air–Ground Task Force Corps always has an ACE (Aviation Combat Element) air arm to back up troops on the ground. One role is to support landings, so the ACE flies jets that can attack enemy aircraft or troops on the ground. The Marines use British-made Harrier jets, which can take off and land vertically from ships.

AV-8B HARRIER jump jets land on a US aircraft carrier.

HARRIER JETS

The Harriers were a Cold War creation. They were designed to take off or land without runways, which would likely be destroyed in a conflict. The Harriers are multirole fighters: they can attack enemy aircraft or strike ground targets.

RANGE OF PLANES

In addition to the Harrier family, Marine pilots fly the F/A-18 Hornet. It provides close air support during air-to-ground attacks. The USMC also has its own transporter aircraft, like the C-130 Hercules, which carry cargo and also parachutists. There are Marine high-altitude surveillance aircraft that listen to enemy electronic communications. The Marines also use unmanned aerial vehicles, or drones, to carry out tactical reconnaissance of enemy territory.

MARINES LOAD a CH-53 helicopter onto a US Air Force C-5 Galaxy cargo plane to take on a mission in East Africa.

AIR FORCE RESERVE COMMAND

HELICOPTERS

As early as 1946 Marine commander and pilot Roy Geiger saw that helicopters would change how the Marines operated. Landings could be made from further away, quicker, and in more force. The helicopter, or chopper, proved its value in Vietnam in the 1960s. Marines could be airlifted straight into combat.

AN MV-22 OSPREY tiltrotor prepares to lift a supply container from the deck of a warship.

CHANGING ROLES

In later conflicts, the role of the chopper grew. It dropped patrols in enemy territory and retrieved them, or airlifted supplies. In Iraq, the Marines used the Cobra AH-1W to strike at insurgents because it fires reliable Hellfire missiles. But the campaign in Afghanistan made Marine bosses reconsider the aircraft's role. The enemy Taliban forces became better at shooting down helicopters with rockets. A big chopper like the Chinook is hard to hide as it lands or takes off.

TILTROTORS

The Marines use tiltrotors, which cross an airplane and a helicopter. A tiltrotor has wings but its thrust comes from rotors. Even though they can take off and land vertically, they are fast and they carry huge loads.

A MARINE rappels out of a UH-1 Huey. Rappelling means a chopper does not even have to land.

SPECIALIST GEAR

Marines fight in all kinds of terrain, including in water, so they need lots of special equipment. But they pride themselves in making old stuff work for them. Often, they buy old equipment from other forces or even foreign armies. They adapt it for whatever they need. USMC has its own armor and artillery, as well as means of transportation.

MARINE artillery gunners fire an M777A2 howitzer; artillery supports all USMC operations.

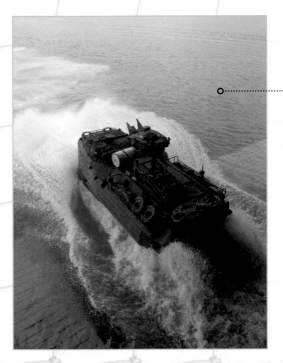

AN AAV leaves the well deck of an amphibious assault ship.

RIDING IN STYLE

The amphibious assault vehicle, or AAV, is a Marine favorite. It powers through the water using a system of water jets. Then it rolls right up onto a beach on its caterpillar tanks. Marines complain that the AAV is noisy, smelly, and cramped. But they also admit that the worst ride is better than the best walk!

LAVs

The light armored vehicle (LAV) carries up to six Marines. It has a cannon, machine guns, and grenade launchers. It is used for air-defense and reconnaissance, as well as combat. It's very easy to maneuver off-road.

MARINES maneuver an AAV during training to join a battalion landing team.

WEAPONS

Marines use different guns and rifles. Close-combat fighting might call for a shotgun, but rifles are more common. Since the 1960s the M16 rifle and its descendants have been the most popular choices. With night vision goggles and an infrared aiming light, Marines can shoot accurately at night.

A SCOUT swimmer sights his M4 carbine as he guards the perimeter of a beach.

EYEWITNESS

"There is a moment when the target disappears, when the shooter sees only the clear, lovely intersection of the reticle [crosshairs], as if a bucket of sun has been poured into his scope, and the light means it's time to pull the trigger."

Anthony Swofford
USMC sniper, Gulf War, 1991

A MARINE aims with his M249 squad automatic weapon (SAW) on a training exercise in Djibouti, in Africa.

SPECIALIST GUNS

A Marine sniper uses a specialist rifle, such as the M40A5 sniper rifle. Snipers have become more and more important in military thinking. Instead of fighting big armies, special forces today often fight smaller groups of terrorists. The M40A5 has a range of up to 1,000 yards (915 m). Machine guns like the M249 SAW are also used to provide suppressing fire that forces the enemy to remain under cover.

GLOSSARY

amphibious (am-FIH-bee-us)
Describes something that works on land and in water; or a landing from the sea on enemy territory.

armor (AR-mer) Battlefield vehicles with protection against enemy fire, like tanks.

artillery (ahr-TIH-lur-ee) Guns that fire large-caliber shells, like cannons, howitzers, or mortars.

battalion (buh-TAL-yun) A large group of soldiers organized as a unit, usually made up of two or more companies.

bayonet (BAY-oh-net) A knifelike blade that is fixed to the muzzle of a rifle and used for close-quarter fighting.

blockade (blah-KAYD) Measures aimed at preventing trade by using ships to intercept vessels heading toward port.

carbine (KAR-been) A light, gas-operated semiautomatic rifle.

expeditionary force
(ek-spuh-DIH-shuh-neh-ree FORS)
An armed force put together for a specific operation overseas.

guerrilla (guh-RIL-uh) Someone who fights through ambushes and sabotage, rather than traditional battles.

hearts and minds (HARTS AND MYNDZ)
A military tactic aimed at winning support by helping a community.

howitzer (HOW-it-ser) A relatively short-barreled cannon that fires shells in a high trajectory.

insurgents (in-SER-jints) Fighters who are revolting against an established government, often by using guerrilla tactics.

martial arts (MAR-shul ARTS) Traditional methods of unarmed combat, such as judo.

rappel (ruh-PEHL) To descend quickly from a helicopter using a rope.

recruits (rih-KROOTS) New members of a group.

Sunset Parade (SUN-set puh-RAYD)
A formal Marine parade that takes place in the evening.

task force (TASK FORS) An armed force put together for a specific operation.

FURTHER READING

Benson, Michael. *The U.S. Marine Corps.* U.S. Armed Forces. Minneapolis, MN: Lerner Classroom, 2005.

Payment, Simone. *Frontline Marines: Fighting in the Marine Combat Arms Units.* Extreme Careers. New York: Rosen Publishing, 2007.

Portman, Michael. *Marine Corps.* US Military Forces. New York: Gareth Stevens, 2012.

Schwartz, Heather. *Women of the Marine Corps: Breaking Barriers.* Mankato, MN: Capstone Press, 2011.

WEBSITES

INDEX